The 'Good' Trees in the Garden
in the Garden

and the Goodness of Jesus

Julie Andrews

Notes –

There are a number of scriptures that refer to the cross as a tree. So I have used cross / tree when my text seem to indicate that the cross could represent the Tree of the Knowledge of Good and Evil. Crucifixion on a wooden cross was a Roman form of execution at the time. This so fits with Jesus dying instead of us.

God is a generally accepted word for our Creator. Although I often use the word "God," better words would be Hebrew names - Elohim, Yahuah, Yahweh, Adonai, or the Name He gave to Moses - "I Am that I Am". Many words explain the depth of our wonderful Creator. I also refer to Him as the triune God - Father, Son (Yeshua, Jesus) and Holy Spirit.

All Scriptures are from the New King James Version unless indicated after the reference.

Dedicated to my family

Julie Andrews 2020

*"And out of the ground the LORD God made every tree grow that is pleasant to the sight and good for food. **The tree of life** was also in the midst of the garden, and **the tree of the knowledge of good and evil.**"*
Genesis 2:9

So what is it about these two trees that makes them different from all the other trees in the garden that were lovely to look at and good for food?

Introduction –

This book is showing the deception Adam fell into by eating from the Tree of the Knowledge of Good and Evil. We are all aware of the evil part of it but what about the good? Good was also included in what God told Adam not to eat. It is part of the same tree that bought a curse, part of the fall of man that brought death.

2 Corinthians 11:3 - *But I fear, lest somehow, as the serpent deceived Eve by his craftiness, so your minds may be corrupted from the simplicity that is in Christ.*

We look at the good part of the Tree of Knowledge and then, having decided that worldly good is from that tree, we discuss how to be set free from this deceit and live in the Kingdom that will have access to the Tree of Life.

I felt our Heavenly Father (Yahweh) said to me - 'worldly goodness is not My good .... Jesus (Yeshua) died on a wooden cross or tree representing the Tree of Knowledge.'

This started me on the discovery that I set out in this book.

When the Father called Abraham to be the father of a special nation and later with Moses who brought Israel out of Egypt, His main aim was that they would be His people and He would be their God. The greatest sin then and still is, is to not love the Lord your God with all your heart. Our greatest work is to love God. Everything else we do stems from that.

Matthew 22:37-38 - *Jesus said to him 'You shall love the LORD your God with all your heart, with all your soul, and with all your mind.' This is the first and great commandment.*

St. Paul writes in Romans 12:2 - *And do not be conformed to this world, but be transformed by the renewing of your mind, that you may prove what is that good and acceptable and perfect will of God.*

He is teaching us that to know what God's good will is we need renewed minds. Fallen mankind is unable to distinguish what is really good, because they are deceived by the Knowledge Tree.

Contents

Chapter 1

The Tree of Life

First we consider the Tree of Life. Adam and Eve were free to eat from this tree and its Life gave them a relationship with God as they were made in His image. They had authority in the earth and would have had eternity with the Creator, fullness of life and all the benefits that brought. They had authority over the created world, creativity naming the animals, companionship and love for each other and a friendship with God walking in the garden. All the other trees in the garden were good for food for our bodies, but the fruit of the Tree of Life was truly good for the whole person, body, soul and spirit.

When God instructed Moses to build the temple He told them to make a lamp-stand called a Menorah and it is thought that this may represent the Tree of Life. (Exodus 25:31-40)

At the end of the Bible in a vision, John saw the Tree of Life.

Revelation 22:2 - *In the middle of its street, and on either side of the river, was the tree of life, which bore twelve fruits, each tree yielding its fruit every month. The leaves of the tree were for the healing of the nations.*

Revelation 22:12 - *"And behold, I am coming quickly, and My reward is with Me, to give to every one according to his work. 14 Blessed are those who do His commandments, that they may have the right to the tree of life, and may enter through the gates into the city.*

It is not clear from the scriptures whether we can actually eat from the Tree of Life before Jesus comes again, but we do have access to everything that Jesus has won for us. He has given us Life in abundance.

John 10:10 - *The thief does not come except to steal, and to kill, and to destroy. I have come that they may have life, and that they may have it more abundantly.*

This Life starts as soon as a person receives Christ Jesus and becomes a new creation, it leads to eternal life now and forever. Jesus has eternally won for us the Fruit of the Tree of Life. It will result in us becoming Christ centered, for it is who we are in Christ that matters and learning how to use His strength and power.

2 Corinthians 5:17 - *Therefore, if anyone is in Christ, he is a new creation; old things have passed away; behold, all things have become new.*

Had Adam and Eve not eaten from the Tree of Knowledge they would have gained their knowledge by the spirit and have been able to use the resources that were created for us all. Everything that is available in this beautiful world would have been revealed to us through our relationship with the Father. We would have creatively discovered electricity for example, probably much earlier maybe in a different form. Everything would have worked in harmony and there would have been no abuse of the Earth. Information would all have come about through our relationship with the spirit and every person would use their creative gifts to the glory of the Father. Only eternity will reveal what we have missed by going our own selfish way. Yet we can have a glimpse of it now. For once we trust our lives to our Saviour Jesus, it opens up the potential of this glorious life.

The gifts and fruit of the spirit are tiny examples of the blessings our Saviour desires to pour upon us. In the ages to come, all who have believed and submitted themselves to the Lord's rule and have a relationship with Him, will be included in His glorious Kingdom for eternity.

James 3:17 – *but the wisdom that is from above is first pure, then peaceable, gentle, willing to yield, full of mercy and good fruits, without partiality and without hypocrisy.*

Chapter 2   The Tree of the Knowledge of Good and Evil.

The Tree of the Knowledge of Good and Evil that Adam was told not to eat from to protect them, brought them knowledge, including evil and death.

Genesis 2:16-17 ... *And the LORD God commanded the man, saying, "Of every tree of the garden you may freely eat; but of the tree of the knowledge of good and evil you shall not eat, for in the day that you eat of it you shall surely die."*

This Tree brought death, not only to mankind but to the whole creation. It caused creation to be cut off from God and become independent and as a result the whole world was affected. Adam and Eve died spiritually when they ate the fruit of the Tree of Knowledge and their bodies started to die. Although they lived for 900 years, the ageing and decaying process started. Their decision meant that the whole of mankind has the DNA of a fallen man subject to decay. It was Lucifer, a fallen angel who became Satan (Revelation 20:2 ...... *the dragon, that serpent of old, who is the Devil and Satan ...*) who plotted and tempted Eve, but she chose to disobey their Creator and Adam did too. This gave Satan the authority that God had given to man.

It was necessary that the Tree of the Knowledge of Good and Evil (knowledge of everything that pertains to the earth) was in the garden, or people would not have had free will. God did not want us to be puppets just trusting in Him because He made us so, He wanted us to be like Him and be free to choose.

The Lord did not put the knowledge tree in Eden to trap people into failure, He wanted them to prove their love, commitment and willingness to obey. If there had been nothing there to test this, then they could not have had the freedom to disobey. With freedom comes responsibility and we have choices to make how we use our freedom. He wanted us to receive knowledge directly from Him rather than being independent of Him. The angels also had choice but sadly Lucifer chose to set up in opposition to God.

Isaiah 14:12 "*How you are fallen from heaven, O Lucifer, son of the morning! ..... For you have said in your heart: 'I will ascend into heaven, I will exalt my throne above the stars of God ...*

In Genesis 3 we read Adam and Eve died because they chose to disobey. They desired and ate from the Tree of the Knowledge of good and evil. They had to be barred from the Tree of Life to stop mankind living in a fallen state for ever.

Genesis 3:22 AMP - *And the LORD God said, "Behold, the man has become like one of Us (Father, Son, Holy Spirit), knowing [how to distinguish between] good and evil; and now, he might stretch out his hand, and take from the tree of life as well, and eat [its fruit], and live [in this fallen, sinful condition] forever"*

But the Father had a plan to rescue mankind should they choose to disobey Him. Jesus, the second Adam, has bought for us, by the price of His precious Blood, access back into the Kingdom that has the Tree of Life.

1 Corinthians 15:22,45,49 - *For as in Adam all die, even so in Christ all shall be made alive... (45) And so it is written, "The first man Adam became a living being." The last Adam became a life-giving spirit. (49) And as we have borne the image of the man of dust, we shall also bear the image of the heavenly Man.*

We also need to know about the evil side of the Tree of the Knowledge of Good and Evil. It is important to understand this, but realise that good and evil are both part of the same Tree that Jesus has delivered us from. Death and dying, evil and sin are the result of being independent and separated from the Life of our Creator. The whole of creation suffered and died as a result of Adam's disobedience, for Adam had authority over creation. Therefore everything was cut off from its Creator. However there will come a time when there will be complete restoration.

Romans 8:18 - 25 - *For I consider that the sufferings of this present time are not worthy to be compared with the glory which shall be revealed in us .... (22) For we know that the whole creation groans and labours with birth pangs together until now ......*

The question, 'why does God allow suffering' is often asked and the reason is that fallen man and Satan are in charge. God gave man authority at the beginning.

Genesis 1:27-28 *So God created man in His own image; in the image of God He created him; male and female He created them. 28 Then God blessed them, and God said to them, "Be fruitful and multiply; fill the earth and subdue it; have dominion over the fish of the sea, over the birds of the air, and over every living thing that moves on the earth."*

This dominion was handed over to Satan by Adam and Eve, and this is the reason for sin and suffering. The devil even tried to get Jesus off course so he will certainly try with us.

Luke 4:5-6 - *Then the devil, taking Him up on a high mountain, showed Him all the kingdoms of the world in a moment of time. (6) And the devil said to Him, "All this authority I will give You, and their glory; for this has been delivered to me, and I give it to whomever I wish."*

Jesus taught that Kingdom living requires dying to self. This is repentance; a turning away from our old selfish, indopondent life and through what Jesus won for us on the cross / tree to find a new life.

Matthew 16:24-25 - *Then Jesus said to His disciples, "If anyone desires to come after Me, let him deny himself, and take up his cross, and follow Me. For whoever desires to save his life will lose it, but whoever loses his life for My sake will find it."*

It is the will of God in both the Old and New Testament that everyone should choose life.

Ezekiel 18:32 - *For I have no pleasure in the death of one who dies," says the Lord GOD. "Therefore turn and live!" and* 1 Timothy 2:3-4 .... *God our Saviour, who desires all men to be saved and to come to the knowledge of the truth.*

Jesus will intervene once the Gospel of the Kingdom has been preached in all the world so everyone has had the opportunity to come to God. (Matthew 24:14) - When Jesus comes again He will *'rule and reign for a thousand years'* (Revelation 20:1-6) after that the last enemy to be defeated is death. Then everything will change for ever. Hallelujah.

1 Corinthians 15:25-26 - *For He must reign till He has put all enemies under His feet. (2) The last enemy that will be destroyed is death.*

Chapter 3 The Great Deception

The independent seed of the fruit of the Tree of Knowledge of Good and Evil is still currently here; but those who freely choose Jesus now belong to Him and should not live influenced by the Knowledge Tree anymore. Satan disguised himself as an angel of light offering greater insight and beguiled Eve with the idea that she would be better off with the wisdom and knowledge that the tree brought.

Genesis 3:5-6 - *For God knows that in the day you eat of it your eyes will be opened, and you will be like God, knowing good and evil." [6] So when the woman saw that the tree was good for food, that it was pleasant to the eyes, and a tree desirable to make one wise, she took of its fruit and ate. She also gave to her husband with her, and he ate.*

The greatest trap of that Tree is the '**Good**' part. Believers are not often tempted by evil but have been taught at home, church and society to live by the good. We usually don't realise it but by living by our own efforts, even the good works we do, can be a stumbling block for true goodness.

Psalm 16:2,11 - *O my soul, you have said to the LORD, "You are my Lord, My goodness is nothing apart from You."*

Jesus is our foundation and all the good works we do are to issue from Him, by the inspiration of the Holy Spirit.

1 Corinthians 3:11-15 - *For no other foundation can anyone lay than that which is laid, which is Jesus Christ. (12) Now if anyone builds on this foundation with gold, silver, precious stones, wood, hay, straw, (13) each one's work will become clear; for the Day will declare it, because it will be revealed by fire; and the fire will test each one's work, of what sort it is. (14) If anyone's work which he has built on it endures, he will receive a reward. (15) If anyone's work is burned, he will suffer loss; but he himself will be saved, yet so as through fire.*

So once we believe and receive Jesus as our Saviour and become a baptised New Creation, our aim should be to live New Creation lives.

Romans 6:4 - *Therefore we were buried with Him through baptism into death, that just as Christ was raised from the dead by the glory of the Father, even so we also should walk in newness of life.*

When we realise that we can't really make the world a better place unless we live from God's Kingdom, it changes our thinking. We pray 'Thy Kingdom come ...', but do we really mean it? Only in the Kingdom will things be better, and eventually be perfect. We currently live in a world that has been spoilt by the seed of the Fruit of Tree of the Knowledge of Good and Evil. Only the Fruit of the Spirit from the Kingdom, with Jesus as the Tree of Life, brings forth good seed and fruit.

Chapter 4   Knowledge and The Law

'The Tree of the Knowledge' was 'knowledge' of good and evil known by God. In His hands that knowledge could do no harm because He is perfect.

Genesis 3:22 - *Then the LORD God said, "Behold, the man has become like one of Us, to know good and evil.*

Adam, made in the image of God was protected by Him and was warned not to eat fruit from that Tree, for God knew that if man became independent it would destroy him. The Law is also for knowing what is right and wrong, good and evil. Both eating that fruit and the Law brought death.

Romans 3:20 - *"since by the law comes knowledge of sin".*

The Law is holy just and good it was given to reveal that sin is sinful.

Romans 7:12-13 - *Therefore the law is holy, and the commandment holy and just and good. (13) Has then what is good become death to me? Certainly not! But sin, that it might appear sin, was producing death in me through what is good, so that sin through the commandment might become exceedingly sinful.*

There are two different covenants, two different ways to come to God, and relate to Him. The Old Covenant is based on our own works and performance.

When Jesus descended to the dead after His crucifixion, He will have granted Life to all those who had done what was lawful and right.

Ezekiel 33:11, 19 - *(11) Say to them: 'As I live,' says the Lord GOD, 'I have no pleasure in the death of the wicked, but that the wicked turn from his way and live. Turn, turn from your evil ways! For why should you die, O house of Israel?' ..... (19) But when the wicked turns from his wickedness and does what is lawful and right, he shall live because of it.*

The New Covenant or Testament is built on the finished work of Jesus on the cross / tree, relating to God through His grace and unconditional love.

The Tree of Knowledge of Good and Evil was a picture of the law and the Old Covenant. Before Adam and Eve ate from the forbidden fruit, they had no knowledge of good and evil. They were innocently unaware of what was morally right or wrongdoing. The result of Adam and Eve eating from the fruit of the Tree of Knowledge of Good and Evil was that man started to relate to God based on his own performance, instead of God's unconditional love. The 'knowledge of good and evil' led to mankind becoming self-righteous and self-reliant when the Israelites said "we can do what God requires":

Exodus 19:7-8 - *So Moses came and called for the elders of the people, and laid before them all these words which the LORD commanded him. (8) Then all the people answered togother and said, "All that the LORD has spoken we will do." So Moses brought back the words of the people to the LORD.*

Because of this God gave the Law to the Jewish people. The 10 Commandments were that Law and they set out God's perfect standard for mankind.
Exodus 20:3 - 17 *"You shall have no other gods before Me ....*

However man was never able to keep the whole law, so it was obvious that they needed a Saviour. Animals were killed, showing only the shedding of blood could remove sin. However, animal sacrifice only lasted for a year whereas Jesus' sacrifice was once and for all people. Nothing more is required except to believe and receive His finished work, turning away from our self reliant old life.

Hebrews 10:10 - *we have been sanctified through the offering of the body of Jesus Christ once for all.*

When Jesus came, He even raised the bar of the law saying for example, 'if a man even looks at a woman lustfully he has committed adultery in his heart.' He was making it obvious that by their own righteousness they could not save themselves. God also gave the Law; because the Israelites had forfeited relationship for knowledge, they chose the Law over Life and self sufficiency over trust.

Therefore Christ came to fulfil the Law and bring us Life. Jesus lived a perfect life thus fulfilling the Law and then He was killed instead of us. This meant we could be forgiven and set free, so were entitled to Life bought for us by Jesus. We receive this Life when we believe what Jesus has won for us and accept His new Life. (This revelation comes in different ways to each one of us)

2 Corinthians 3:5-6 AMP   *...our sufficiency and qualifications come from God.*
(6) He has qualified us [making us sufficient] as ministers of a new covenant [of salvation through Christ], not of the letter [of a written code] but of the Spirit; for the letter [of the Law] kills [by revealing sin and demanding obedience], but the Spirit gives life.

Once Jesus had died and risen for us, He fulfilled the Law and broke the curse of the Tree of Knowledge.

Galatians 3:13 NLT *But Christ has rescued us from the curse pronounced by the law. When he was hung on the cross, he took upon himself the curse for our wrongdoing. For it is written in the scriptures "cursed is everyone who is hung on a tree"*

Mankind was free again should they choose new Life; then they will have fellowship with the Father and will live forever in His presence.

Chapter 5 - What are God's Thoughts on Good and Evil?

God is good – Psalm 100:5 - *For the Lord is good: His mercy is everlasting, And His truth endures to all generations.*

I felt Our Heavenly Father said 'worldly goodness is not My good; your goodness, is not My good. My good is the Fruit of the Spirit (Galatians 5:22-23). My good lives in fellowship with Me and others. My good has righteous authority over evil. My good depends on Me to bring healing, miracles and other supernatural spiritual gifts. It does not need to strive because it is trusting in My provision. My good is found in the Tree of Life that I won for you by the shedding of the precious blood of My Son, Jesus (Yeshua). His blood paid the redemption price when He hung on a cross representing the Tree of the Knowledge of Good and Evil, He died on a tree to buy you back and set you free from that Tree.'

1 Peter 2:24 .... *who Himself bore our sins in His own body on the tree, that we, having died to sins, might live for righteousness-by whose stripes you were healed.*

Acts 13:29 - *Now when they had fulfilled all that was written concerning Him, they took Him down from the tree and laid Him in a tomb.*

Galatians 3:13 - *Christ has redeemed us from the curse of the law, having become a curse for us (for it is written, "Cursed is everyone who hangs on a tree"),*

So because Jesus was put to death on a wooden cross, all the goodness and evil of that Knowledge Tree has been put to death for those who believe. He paid the death penalty so you could be delivered'. "you were bought at a price"

1Corinthians 6:20 and 7:23 - *For you were bought at a price; therefore glorify God in your body and in your spirit, which are God's.*

The price was Jesus's precious Blood, so now we belong to Him. The fruit of the Spirit will issue from everyone who has been bought through Jesus and lives close to Him.

Galatians 5:22-23 - *But the fruit of the Spirit is love, joy, peace, longsuffering, kindness, goodness, faithfulness, 23 gentleness, self-control. Against such there is no law.*

God is a good God of love but also a God of justice, this is something we need to be aware of. He wants everyone to have life, He wants everyone to be saved and live to their full potential. Sadly there are many who deliberately choose not only to decide for themselves that they want to remain independent from God, but are set on preventing other people from knowing the truth.
This is why Jesus was so hard on the Pharisees. They were supposed to be drawing people to the Father but they had set up their own rules and regulations that were not according to the Father's heart and they confused others and stopped them entering the Kingdom. He accused them of having the devil as their

father. God's justice dealt with evil when Jesus was punished in our place. But those who refuse to accept Jesus's sacrifice on their behalf do not benefit from what Jesus has done for us. So when He comes again, Jesus will come with a sword and evil will have to be destroyed.

Revelation 19:11 - *Now I saw heaven opened, and behold, a white horse. And He who sat on him was called Faithful and True, and in righteousness He judges and makes war.*

If that did not happen then mankind would be doomed forever to live under the power of the Tree of the Knowledge of Good and Evil. Satan will be bound for a thousand years during the 'millennium' rule and reign of Jesus on earth. But currently we are in the covenant of grace, for the love, mercy and compassion of God, who is longing for as many people as possible to come into His Kingdom. It is so sad that people do not see what they are missing by being independent of their loving, Heavenly Father. We are not to judge other people because only God sees into people's hearts and knows what they are really like. He is aware of all that they have been through in their lives and why they behave in the ways that they do. So we do not judge our loved ones or anybody else as eternally unsaved, because we never know others completely. We are to love and pray for them, tell and demonstrate to them the love of God by showing what He is really like. We should explain about Jesus and His Kingdom, then commit them to the loving mercy of God.

Chapter 6   How can I Transfer Trees?

When you come to Jesus like a dependent and trusting little child, desiring to be set free from independent worldly Knowledge of good as well as evil, you identify with Jesus. By faith you have become one with Him. Jesus said several times in John 14 to 17 that we are one with Him and are to **abide** in Him. This is how we need to live believing it is true, not just a vague thought belief, but a relationship with the Father through unity with Jesus and what He has won for us on the cross / tree. Have a sure and certain hope that Jesus' blood was shed in place of ours. There is Life in the Blood. We may not fully realise what took place on that cross, representing the tree, nobody fully understands, but we do need to make a personal response. Jesus paid the price for our freedom by the death penalty, so that we could be delivered from the death curse of the Tree of the Knowledge of Good and Evil.

Many Christians stick with the basics, they spend their lives believing that because of Jesus they will be forgiven of any wrongdoing when they repent, but still living mainly in the Tree of the Knowledge of Good, even if they are mainly freed from the 'evil' part. The good of that tree is our human goodness but though inspired by Jesus' example, we try to copy Jesus **in our own strength** so it is still independent of the Father.

Much of the teaching in church is challenging us to work hard to live good, moral lives rather than new creation lives dependent on the Father. Jesus Christ said "*I have come that you might have life and live it to the full*" (John 10:10, 17, 27). Jesus laid down His life for us, so we become His sheep, or as James 1:1 says; bondservant. He leads us and we follow. The 'independent good' as well as the 'evil' needs to die.

Matthew 16:24 *Then Jesus said to His disciples, "If anyone desires to come after Me, let him deny himself, and take up his cross, and follow Me*

However, Jesus died on our behalf so when we unite with Jesus we become one with His death and resurrection. We are a new creation in our spirit, as Jesus has done everything necessary to make us redeemed, washed, forgiven, healed and much more. Our mind and our body still need to be renewed, so we come to realise what Jesus has done for us. We will be transformed "from glory to glory." This indicates an unfolding process to change us into His image. We submit to it by "beholding the glory of the Lord." As we behold His glory, we will be changed into His image.

2 Corinthians 3:18 - *But we all, with unveiled face, beholding as in a mirror*
the glory of the Lord, are being transformed into the same image from
glory to glory, just as by the Spirit of the Lord.

We recognise that we cannot earn our salvation and we accept what the scriptures say about that (verse 8 below) - for by grace we are saved. Yet we often do not see that we should go on to verses 9 and 10 below that say He has prepared good works especially for us.

Ephesians 2:8 -10 *For by grace you have been saved through faith, and that*
not of yourselves; it is the gift of God, (9) *not of works, lest anyone should boast.* (10) *For we are His workmanship,* **created in Christ Jesus for good works**, *which God prepared beforehand that we should walk in them*

We do not have to keep on trying to prove ourselves to God and other people that by our good works we are living a good Christian life. What we should be doing from this time forward is doing the 'good works' by the grace of God, united to Jesus, abiding in Him. In the same way that Jesus demonstrated and said -

John 5:19 "*Most assuredly, I say to you, the Son can do nothing of Himself, but what He sees the Father do; for whatever He does, the Son also does in like manner.*"

We are called to be dead to this world because of the sacrifice of Jesus -

Galatians 6:14 *But God forbid that I should boast except in the cross of our*
Lord Jesus Christ, by whom the world has been crucified to me, and I to the world.

The 'Good' Trees in the Garden: and the Goodness of Jesus

Paperback – 27 Nov. 2020

by Julie Andrews (Author)

> See all formats and editions

Kindle Edition	Paperback
£1.99	£4.00

Read with Our Free App

1 New from £4.00

Arrives: Saturday, Dec 19 Details

Fastest delivery: Tuesday, Dec 15

Order within 21 hrs 52 mins Details

Note: This **item is eligible for click and collect.** Details

This book shows the deception that Adam fell into by eating of the Tree of the Knowledge of Good and Evil. Good was also included in what God told Adam not to eat, it is part of the tree that brought the fall of man and death.I felt our Heavenly Father say to me 'worldly goodness is not My good ...... Jesus died on a wooden cross or tree representing the Tree of Knowledge.' This started me on the discovery that I set out in this book.

This is a 55 page booklet on the 'Good' part of the tree of the Knowledge of Good and Evil and how when Jesus died on the cross that it represented this tree.

They are available on Amazon in Book or Kindle format and I have copies here that I could post to you. contact - julie.a.m.andrews@gmail.co.uk or phone 01903740405 leaving your details.   Proceeds to charity.

What can the world do to a dead man? A dead man does not feel rejected, abused, taken advantage of or have concern for the world's problems. If we consider daily what Jesus won for us on the cross / tree and tell Him about them we would be set free of the worries and entanglements of this world. Let go and let God motivate our lives.

The Christian life is not about us – it's all about Christ... it's about putting God's will over our will... it's about putting Christ first above everything else.

Matthew 16:24-25 - *Then Jesus said to His disciples, "If anyone desires to come after Me, let him deny himself, and take up his cross, and follow Me. For whoever desires to save his life will lose it, but whoever loses his life for My sake will find it.*

This all sounds very hard and not very enjoyable, lots of giving up and self control. This will be the case unless we can experience that living in the Kingdom is even more exciting than living in the world. The individual who "dies to self" understands that God created him for a reason; that he is a part of God's plan for the world. To be used of God one needs to understand who we really are in Christ, and how it is that God can use us. Jesus endured the cross because He knew that it was going to bring Him great joy in the future.

Hebrews 12:2 - ... *who for the joy that was set before Him endured the cross, despising the shame, and has sat down at the right hand of the throne of God.*

Somehow we have to look beyond what we currently experience, to all the benefits of the Kingdom. At first all of this may not seem very appealing. What about having fun? I believe the Lord does want us to have fun and to enjoy our lives. He blesses us and has created the earth richly for us to enjoy and live in with all of its wonderful blessings. He gives us good gifts, He gives us one another to love and receive love. Consider what God has blessed us with and who He is. He has given us a sense of humour so He must be a fun loving God. He made many weird and wonderful creatures so I believe that was just having fun with His creation. He gave us many gifts to make music, to dance and be sporty, to be creative through art and craft, through poetry and creative stories, even to be good at mathematics – my husband who enjoyed maths often said 'God was a mathematician'. So much of creation is very beautiful for us to enjoy, just to give us pleasure. He gave us wine to make the heart glad, beautifying ointments and delicious tasting food to keep us healthy.

Psalm 104:15 - ... *And wine that makes glad the heart of man, Oil to make his face shine, And bread which strengthens man's heart.*

Love is His greatest value and He gave Adam and Eve the joy of having children together, the sexual act, as well as the pleasure that our families can bring. We are also given friends, animals as pets and many wonderful things to love and bring us joy and happiness.

1 Corinthians 13:13 *And now abide faith, hope, love, these three;*
but the greatest of these is love.

We do not lose these things by loving God and living in the Kingdom and the Kingdom of heaven promises to be even more wonderful. We have the marriage supper of the Lamb (Revelation 19:9) to look forward to and that sounds amazing.

However it can be hard to get ourselves out of the world. What we need to do is to get more into the Kingdom and then the worldly way will seem less attractive. What could possibly be more exciting than to have fellowship with the Almighty? What could possibly be more interesting?

John 15:11 *"These things I have spoken to you, that My joy may remain in you, and that your joy may be full.*

Chapter 7   What about all the Good Kind Things Christians Do?

It is not about sitting around not doing anything waiting for God to speak to us. Of course we should be doing good works and the Father expects us to use our natural abilities. These precious gifts are entrusted to us and He wants us to use them for His glory. Many lovely believers use their gifts in wonderful ways. He has gifted us with a vast range of abilities and talents that are to be used in His service. The parable of the talents shows that we are expected to use our talents for His glory.

Exodus 31:2-5 - *"See, I have called by name Bezalel ... And I have filled him with the Spirit of God, in wisdom, in understanding, in knowledge, and in all manner of workmanship, to design artistic works, to work in gold, in silver, in bronze, in cutting jewels for setting, in carving wood, and to work in all manner of workmanship.*

You may feel confused as it sounds as if being a good person might be done by your own strength and all your efforts have been in vain. God says *"I see your heart and that you desire goodness. That is a stepping stone to My goodness, just learn to come and ask Me to help you and give you the grace to live in pure goodness and strength".*

All our good works are good. He wants us to do good works and if in our hearts we are doing them because God is good, and we want to be like Jesus and if that is our motivation, then He sees and loves that. However, when we learn to listen to the Holy Spirit prompting, showing us what our Father is doing, then this is an even better way. Most of the time we live a mixture, because we are growing in our faith - being changed from glory to glory. But in order to see miracles we need to see and do what the Father wants us to do and then act upon what we see. This was how Jesus operated. The Father is looking for the likeness of His Son in us. By reading the Bible we learn more about what God's will is, and as we live in His presence the Holy Spirit prompts us so we somehow know what to do.

All your goodness has been appreciated by those who you have helped and it has not been in vain. But have there been times when you have known that you did not have enough strength to be as good as you wanted to be? It is not the acts that were wrong, it was the **trying in your own strength** to do them. There were those times when you knew that God had prompted you to do something for someone else, then when you did it that time, it was easier and brought more fruit. But there will have been other times when you acted because you felt you ought to, or someone asked you and you didn't like to say no, or you were made to feel guilty if you didn't.   Your goodness might have been manipulated by others for their advantage, or an employers gain or for the benefit of a church programme. Other times you did good things because it made you feel happy, or just to make someone else feel happy. This is a lovely motive but it's source may have been the good part of the tree of Knowledge. When your actions glorify you rather than the Father, then it does not draw others into the Kingdom. It's still good, it just may not be God's best.

A friend said she commits her day to the Lord and trusts she is doing His will. This is right and basically it is between each individual and the Father as to how we work this out. If we have joy and peace within, whatever we are doing, then we can trust it is His good.

Colossians 3:17 - *And whatever you do in word or deed, do all in the name of the Lord Jesus, giving thanks to God the Father through Him.*
23 - And whatever you do, do it heartily, as to the Lord and not to men,

If when doing things we are stressed, angry, fearful or have any negative thoughts, then we should talk to the Holy Spirit about it and if necessary change what we are doing. This is true with a job. Sometimes the Lord says 'endure this, I can use it to your benefit' – then we may learn through problems, for our attitude can change things.   Other times it is right to say no and move on. Most of the time we just get on with life without really thinking. Yet deep down there can be peace or stress, joy or frustration and our minds and bodies do know the difference and react accordingly.

1 Thessalonians 5: 15 -18 - *... pursue what is good both for yourselves and for all. Rejoice always, pray without ceasing, in everything give thanks; for this is the will of God in Christ Jesus for you.*

Let's be happy and joyful whatever we are doing. It might be shopping, being at work, cooking or just going about our everyday life. It is not a matter of changing our actions, wondering whether we should be doing this or that, these things probably need to be done. it is changing the heart spirit behind the action. Everything can be done in either a selfish way or a Godly way. Yet self-analysis over this would be feeding self. It's just a change of heart whereby we bless the Lord, thank and praise Him - not because we ought to but because we want to.

Psalm 34:1- *I will bless the LORD at all times; His praise shall continually be in my mouth.*

When we go about our life carrying worry, fear, greed, boredom or selfish anger, then we are living with negative emotions. We might be doing the same things, but when we do them with delight, peace, joy, thankfulness and praise, they become a blessing and we have a godly heart emotion. This is a change in our will and heart; not our actions. And it's not about working hard, trying to become different, it's knowing that because of Jesus we are already a new creation. It can take a while to grasp this and it is what Paul meant when he wrote in Romans 12, quoted at the end of this chapter about the renewal of the mind. Most of us just change naturally as we grow in our knowledge and love of God and come to realise all the wonderful things He has done for us.

If we find ourselves burdened by worry as we go about our daily work, then once we realise this we must turn it round and thank God for good things. Above all else we thank God for being our Saviour and friend, our ever present help in trouble, who will never leave us or forsake us. If we are in pain and cannot muster the strength to do that, we need a brother or sister in Christ to support us and pray for us that we might be strong again.

Matthew 11:28-30 - *Come to Me, all you who labor and are heavy laden, and I will give you rest. 29 Take My yoke upon you and learn from Me, for I am gentle and lowly in heart, and you will find rest for your souls. 30 For My yoke is easy and My burden is light."*

Jesus's yoke is to do the Father's will. He does not want us to be exhausted and stressed trying and working hard to cope. He wants us to rest in His love and peace. We may be doing more than is necessary and we need His wisdom to discern what is essential and what can be left.

James 3:13,17 - Who is wise and understanding among you? Let him show
by good conduct that his works are done in the meekness of wisdom. 17 But the wisdom that is from above is first pure, then peaceable, gentle, willing to yield, full of mercy and good fruits, without partiality and without hypocrisy.

To overcome and do good works in His strength; practice the presence of God. Speak in the spirit to Father and allow Him to transform you and renew your mind. Walk in faith not in self.

Romans 12:2 *And do not be conformed to this world, but be transformed by the renewing of your mind, that you may prove what is that good and acceptable and perfect will of God.*

Chapter 8 - God's Goodness and the World's Goodness.

God's goodness can be summed up by the fruit of the Spirit. Love, joy, peace, longsuffering, kindness, goodness, faithfulness, gentleness and self-control. It is these qualities that should be seen in our lives. We do need the Holy Spirit to enable us to be fruitful.

The good works we do, when done in Jesus' Name with Him beside us, will have greater power and glorify the Father. We cannot save ourselves and we need to live our new lives in His strength. It is obvious from some scriptures that to do the supernatural works of Jesus, we need the Holy Spirit to perform them through us. Then we cannot boast, but humbly know that it is not by our own power or ability that we work the miracles of God. When we are convinced that we cannot do certain things in our own strength, it causes us to rely on the Holy Spirit and then we know our need of God.

Titus 3:5 *not by works of righteousness which we have done, but according to His mercy He saved us, through the washing of regeneration and renewing of the Holy Spirit.*
John 14:12-13 - "*Most assuredly, I say to you, he who believes in Me, the works that I do he will do also; and greater works than these he will do, because I go to My Father. [13] And whatever you ask in My name, that I will do, that the Father may be glorified in the Son.*

It is the evil part of the Tree of Knowledge that easily destroys people. Satan knows this, so he is aware that good people are harder to destroy, as he is a deceiver and he masquerades as an angel of light -

2 Corinthians 11:14 *And no wonder! For Satan himself transforms himself into an angel of light.*

Once people become Christians the deceiver tries at all costs to make them trust in their own strength and goodness, rather than discover God's enabling goodness. This will wear out a kind person so they have no time to seek God. He also deceives good, well-meaning but unconverted people to trust in their own goodness and think that, if there is a God He will accept them because of their good works. Most world religions and cults trust in their own actions to earn salvation by being approved of and accepted of their god.

Man thinks being good is important as they understand 'good' is the right way. Yet what one person thinks is good another may not. Different cultures have very different values of what is good, in fact many today with political correctness are calling good evil and evil good.

Isaiah 5:20 – *woe to those who call good evil and evil good;*

Christians can be very influenced by their culture and we need discernment to know the truth of many situations. We need God's wisdom to put His Word first if it clashes with what the world is saying. God gave the Israelites the Law to show His standards and they thought that they were good enough to keep it. But as we saw earlier, God really gave the law in order that it would show Israel that they would not be able to obey it and that they needed a Saviour.

Hebrews 7:19 - *for the law made nothing perfect; on the other hand, there is the bringing in of a better hope, through which we draw near to God.*

Only Jesus was able to keep the law and He came to show us how we could also do the same. He fully obeyed it on our behalf so that we could be delivered and be remade like Him. We can only do this as we learn to abide in Him.

Chapter 9   So How do we Stay in Jesus in the Kingdom?

Abide in Jesus

John 15: 3 - 5 *Abide in Me, and I in you. As the branch cannot bear fruit of itself, unless it abides in the vine, neither can you, unless you abide in Me.*
5 "I am the vine, you are the branches. He who abides in Me, and I in him,
bears much fruit; for without Me you can do **nothing***.*

Jesus explained that those who belong to Him are cleansed, but in order to live in Him they must abide. **The Holy Spirit was sent to help us.** Without being in Him we can do nothing. We sometimes don't recognise that we need to transfer to the Kingdom, with the Tree of Life, and the only way to do that is to stay in Jesus, listen to the Father and live by trusting dependence on the resurrection power of the Holy Spirit. We need to tell our mind and body to agree with our new creation, changed spirit. No longer do we have to be in the Tree of Knowledge we have been transferred by Jesus to Life, Hallelujah!

Romans 5:17 *For if by the one man's offence death reigned through the one,*
much more those who receive abundance of grace and of the gift of righteousness will reign in life through the One, Jesus Christ.

So if by our unity with Jesus we have died to our old life, we also by our unity in Him are resurrected.

Romans 6:3 - 6, ... 5 *For if we have been united together in the likeness of His death, certainly we also shall be in the likeness of His resurrection, ...* Then we live in the Kingdom that we have often asked the Father for - '*Thy Kingdom come, Thy will be done on earth as it is in heaven*'.

Every genuine child of God wants to be used by God to accomplish His will in the world. Jesus said in the Gospel of John 15:8 *"By this My Father is glorified, that you bear much fruit, and so prove to be My disciples"*. That is the essence of God's plan - we are saved to bear fruit; created in Christ Jesus for good works.

Ephesians 2:10 - **For we are His workmanship, created in Christ Jesus for good works, which God prepared beforehand that we should walk in them.**

We bear fruit when Christ lives His life in and through us. Often life does not turn out as we want, life can be difficult for us and for the ones we love. We really cannot manage on our own and we are not expected to. It was not easy for Jesus but despite difficulties He overcame and when we abide in Him we will too.

John 14: 16 .. *I will pray the Father, and He will give you another helper, that He may abide with you forever – the Spirit of truth …*

Galatians 2:20 KJV - *I am crucified with Christ: nevertheless I live; yet not I,*
but Christ liveth in me: and the life which I now live in the flesh I live by
the faith of the Son of God, who loved me, and gave himself for me.

The apostle Paul said, "*For me, to live is Christ, and to die is gain*" (Phil 1:21). The Lord wants us to live a godly and spiritually productive happy life.

The Bible gives us words and promises, but it is just head knowledge if it is not brought alive by the Holy Spirit. We have to go beyond knowing doctrine. We grow in our relationship through prayer and worship, by talking to God. Speaking in a language that the Holy Spirit has given us especially helps us to take what is in our heads and make it alive in our hearts, it makes the words personal. (If you do not have a spiritual language then worship in your own language and it may well lead to this blessing).

First we must minister to Jesus and this will help us to get everything right. We are usually so keen to just use Him to minister to ourselves and to others, but first we should spend time in His presence loving Him. That is the first commandment - *love the Lord your God with all your heart*... After that the Lord can use us to help other people and '*love our neighbours as ourselves*'.

The level of power in our lives is directly related to the level of intimacy we have with Him. But we must take care that our motives are right, that we are not having intimacy in order to get something from God. We should be intimate because we love our Saviour with all our heart.

We need to love and worship Him and seek Christ-likeness as our chief goal, then He can then trust us with His authority. We are called to be like Jesus but we will probably find as Jesus did, that we are not understood and will be like aliens mentioned in 1Peter 2:11, or be like strangers and pilgrims as the Old Testament people of faith.

Hebrews 11:13 - *These all died in faith, not having received the promises,*
but having seen them afar off were assured of them, embraced them
and confessed that they were strangers and pilgrims on the earth.

So as we abide and trust in Jesus may our Father keep us secure and work His life into us, so we may have confidence that we are doing his will.

Hebrews 13:21 - ... *make you complete in every good work to do His will, working in you what is well pleasing in His sight, through Jesus Christ, to whom be glory forever and ever. Amen.*

Chapter 10 - Jesus Always Operated from the Tree of Life

Jesus always operated from the Tree of Life so we need to choose to let go and die to the Tree of Knowledge with it's independent spirit, and claim the victory Jesus has bought for us by His precious Blood. Submit, by letting go of control of our own lives and live as Jesus did, by listening to the Father and doing only what we see He is doing.

John 5:19 ... *"Most assuredly, I say to you, the Son can do nothing of Himself, but what He sees the Father do; for whatever He does, the Son also does in like manner. 20 For the Father loves the Son, and shows Him all things that He Himself does;*
John 14:10 - *..... I am in the Father, and the Father in Me. The words that I speak to you I do not speak on my own authority; but the Father who dwells in Me does the works.*

The Father sent Jesus to live as a man so that we would have a pattern and example. He is able to judge mankind because He has lived His life as a man and therefore is worthy to judge.

John 5:30 - *I can of Myself do nothing. As I hear, I judge; and My judgment is righteous, because I do not seek My own will but the will of the Father who sent Me.*

Jesus entered this world as a miraculous baby born of a virgin mother. He grew up as a normal child and aged 12, He studied under the Rabbis. Before His ministry He must have spent much time studying the Scriptures. His miraculous ministry however, did not start until the Holy Spirit came upon Him at His Baptism. Then the Spirit led Jesus into the desert for a time of preparation. Satan attempted to get Him off course, but using the Scriptures He overcame the temptation. His ministry included compassionate healing, miraculous provision, teaching the truth about the Kingdom and challenging those who distorted the Scriptures. He gathered a group of followers together and taught them to go out and minister by healing the sick and preaching about the Kingdom.

Jesus is the role model sent by the Father to show us how to live in the way that we were designed; to dwell in fellowship with God..

Philippians 2:5,7-8,13 - *Let this mind be in you which was also in Christ Jesus ......7 but made Himself of no reputation, taking the form of a bondservant, and coming in the likeness of men. 8 And being found in appearance as a man He humbled Himself ....*

The Father is looking for the likeness of His Son in us. As we saw in the previous chapter Jesus sent His Holy Spirit to enable us; and we need to cooperate with the Holy Spirit in order to live as Jesus did.

When in the garden of Gethsemane Jesus sweat drops of blood, knowing that He was going to be sacrificed because that is what He came to do. He asked the Father if there was any other way, because He knew the pain He was going to have inflicted upon Him, (although I think it was worse than even He could possibly have imagined). However, He submitted to the Father in order to save us and when people saw Him lifted up on the cross as a man, they would know that He was the Saviour Messiah. They did not see it at first, but afterwards they understood and then, those who believed knew that He was the Messiah. We also understand this when we study carefully and see, what Jesus went through for us. We then perceive that it had to be done in order that sin could be judged in Jesus, to pay the penalty for sin and set us free. He is the Messiah, the Saviour of the world.

John 8:28 - *Then Jesus said to them, "When you lift up the Son of Man, then you will know that I am He, and that I do nothing of Myself; but as My Father taught Me, I speak these things.*

Chapter 11   The Choice of Living in the Kingdom

If we decide to remain independent, mainly in charge of our own lives, living in the Tree of Knowledge most of the time we open ourselves up to Satan's attack. We are out of the full protection of the Father, though the Holy Spirit within is nudging and prompting us to go Jesus's way. We often find ourselves having to repent. Basically the victory has already been won by Jesus for our triumph over sin, sickness and all Satan's lies. We need to willingly die to our selfish desires and own plans; even our well meaning good works done to impress God, others and ourselves. We should let go of controlling our own lives and live in submission to the Father in Jesus' Name.

Romans 6:4   - *Therefore we were buried with Him through baptism into death, that just as Christ was raised from the dead by the glory of the Father,*
even so we also should walk in newness of life.

We shouldn't do good because it seems like a good idea, or even because we are a naturally nice person, (though God does use our personality gifts to bring glory to Him) we should do the works which God has prepared for us to do.

Ephesians 2:10 *For we are His workmanship, created in Christ Jesus for good works, which God prepared beforehand that we should walk in them*

Now this means living by reliance on the Holy Spirit and it is not something we naturally do at first. We have been taught to be a 'good' person by our parents, school, church, friends and others. But so have non-Christians and that is why we do not stand out as being different because we are actually no better in our own strength than a non-Christian. In fact many kind unbelievers can outdo Christians by good works because they are just naturally nice good people. This makes it hard to evangelise to a good person because they think that if there is a God their good works will earn them salvation. It is also why all the different religions place living a good moral life as the key to being accepted by their god. Christianity is different, it is what God has already done for us in Jesus, not what I do for God by myself.

God made us and all of creation in the first place, and then when people chose to go the wrong way He took all that was in us of the Tree of the Knowledge of Good and Evil and put it to death in His own Son. Then The Father brought Jesus alive again so mankind can also be made alive again in Him. To benefit from this gift people just have to believe Jesus died for them, turn away from (repent of) their independent old life and choose to become a child of God. God then makes them a New Creation in Christ Jesus. It's all about what He has done for us, not what we do for Him.

1 Corinthians 3:11-15 - *For no other foundation can anyone lay than that which is laid, which is Jesus Christ. (2) Now if anyone builds on this foundation with gold, silver, precious stones, wood, hay, straw, (13) each one's work will become clear; for the Day will declare it, because it will be revealed by fire; and the fire will test each one's work, of what sort it is. (14) If anyone's work which he has built on it endures, he will receive a reward. (15) If anyone's work is burned, he will suffer loss; but he himself will be saved, yet so as through fire.*

It took the Israelites 40 years to get slavery in Egypt out of their lives and culture. Even then, following generations were lured by the false gods of other nations and failed to benefit from the Promised Land that God had given them. It can also take us many years before we get the old life out of ourselves, it is usually a growing experience. Once we know what is going on it is our choice, how quickly we do this. Over the centuries few Christians have grasped this because they have not been taught correctly. False teachers have led the church and misled the people. The Reformation started to put this right but reform was not taken far enough and even today most believers are not aware of all that our Saviour has won for us.

As the author of this booklet I am aware that we are in a battle. It is a growing awareness and most of us are part way there; it is a journey. The enemy does not want us to overcome and grasp what Jesus has done for us. Over the centuries Satan has done a really good job of convincing the 'church' that living a good life in one's own strength is the way to please God. We have been programmed throughout our lives to live either in a secular way, or if we are believers, in a busy way, doing our best to be a good person.

Romans 8:5,11 - *For those who live according to the flesh set their minds on the things of the flesh, but those who live according to the Spirit, the things of the Spirit. [11] But if the Spirit of Him who raised Jesus from the dead dwells in you, He who raised Christ from the dead will also give life to your mortal bodies through His Spirit who dwells in you.*

Any change does not take place overnight, although for the believer in theory it has already taken place. Our spirit has been changed because of what Jesus won for us; otherwise we could not be confident that we are saved and forgiven; but our minds and bodies need to come into line with our spirits in order to live like Jesus. This is the dichotomy of the Christian life, and most believers give up because they think it is their battle. But it is not our battle, Jesus has already won the victory we just need to come into agreement with what He has already done.

1 John 5:4-5 - *For whatever is born of God overcomes the world.*
And this is the victory that has overcome the world-our faith. 5 Who is he who
overcomes the world, but he who believes that Jesus is the Son of God?

Realising the victory is already won does make the process easier, but it is still something that often takes a long time to put into practice. This is the believers lifetime journey of discovery and transformation, and it is an exciting one.

2 Corinthians 3:18 - *But we all, with unveiled face, beholding as in a mirror*
the glory of the Lord, are being transformed into the same image
from glory to glory, just as by the Spirit of the Lord.

Chapter 12   Living the New Creation Life in God's Goodness.

Living a New Creation life starts with a choice. It is hard to let go of going our own way, but if we do, it brings the love, joy and peace that we really desire. In His presence is fullness of joy. It will, as Jesus and the early believers discovered and experienced, bring opposition, because worldly people do not like holiness and righteousness. They will persuade and revile to try and bring us down. Those in the Tree of Knowledge will always persecute those in the Kingdom with the Tree of Life; Jesus and the Apostles all spoke of this - 2Timothy 3:12 ... *those who live a godly life in Christ Jesus will be persecuted.* So the Christian believer, unless dedicated and firm can get drawn back for a placid life. Yet there is Holy Spirit power available in the Kingdom and also love, peace, freedom and joy.

Oh how thankful we should be and how much we will worship our Father in heaven. We sing songs and hymns that glorify Him. Speak out with a thankful, grateful and loving heart. Spend time in the Lord's presence and worship Him until we know that the world does not have the same attraction to us as we once thought. This can take a long time to develop, but as long as we are growing in our new life, we just keep going. Until we truly do the works He has prepared for us; that should be our aim.

Philippians 3:9 ... *and be found in Him, not having my own righteousness, which is from the law, but that which is through faith in Christ, the righteousness which is from God by faith.*

It is not so much that the works themselves will be different but it is the motivation and the spirit behind them. Jesus always worked from a heart of compassion and He only did what He saw His Father doing. What we really want to see is what we read about in the book of Acts, when people were healed and converted so they came to know the Lord Jesus Christ. These first believers were inspired by Peter's sermon.

Acts 2:17-21 - *'And it shall come to pass in the last days, says God, That I will pour out of My Spirit on all flesh; Your sons and your daughters shall prophesy, Your young men shall see visions, Your old men shall dream dreams. (18) And on My menservants and on My maidservants I will pour out My Spirit in those days; And they shall prophesy.*
(19) I will show wonders in heaven above And signs in the earth beneath: Blood and fire and vapour of smoke. (20) The sun shall be turned into darkness, And the moon into blood, Before the coming of the great and awesome day of the LORD. (21) And it shall come to pass that whoever calls on the name of the LORD Shall be saved.'

Before the Lord comes again we will see Jesus's prophecy taking place.

Matthew 24:14 - *And this gospel of the kingdom will be preached in all the world as a witness to all the nations, and then the end will come.*

There have been times when people have lived like this over the two millennia since Jesus walked this earth. The early Moravians were examples of this yet they were persecuted for believing the truth of the Bible and following the example of the first disciples. However they went out into the world as Jesus instructed His followers and made many disciples.

Matthew 28:18-20 - *And Jesus came and spoke to them, saying, "All authority has been given to Me in heaven and on earth. Go therefore and make disciples of all the nations, baptising them in the name of the Father and of the Son and of the Holy Spirit, teaching them to observe all things that I have commanded you; and lo, I am with you always, even to the end of the age."*

May we His current-day disciples, finish this great commission to go into all the world; healing the sick, bringing deliverance and preaching the Gospel of the Kingdom as Jesus did. We will be bearing the fruit of the Spirit of the Tree of Life and will bring life and light to many people. As believers we need to be strong and firm in our faith as we see the world getting darker. We will shine as lights in this needy world. After drawing as many people as possible into the Kingdom, Jesus will come again for His glorious bride the 'Ecclesia'. (Church). He will then rule and reign for a thousand years (Revelation 20)

Matthew 5:16 - *Let your light so shine before men, that they may see your*
good works and glorify your Father in heaven.

When we realise that Jesus has done so much for us, we cannot help but follow Him. For He left His glory in Heaven to be born in humility, lived a perfect human life and then suffered and died in our place.

Philippians 2:7-8 - *He made Himself of no reputation, taking the form of a bondservant, and coming in the likeness of men. [8] And being found in appearance as a man, He humbled Himself and became obedient to the point of death, even the death of the cross.*

Jesus' endured the betrayal, the lies spoken against Him, the scourging, tearing the flesh from His back, the crown of thorns rammed on His head, the ridicule, the nails piercing His hands that had healed the sick; He suffered the crucifixion on a wooden tree / cross and the torment of being separated from His Father, so that we can become new creations in Him.

Jesus has bought us back with His precious blood, He has paid the price to set us free from the Tree of Knowledge. He has healed us by the wounds inflicted on His dear body. He has been judged instead of us.

We have peace with God and have had our fellowship with Him restored. We have been given new Life and placed in His Kingdom, so that we can live with Him for eternity, starting now. He has sent His Holy Spirit so we are empowered to be as Jesus was in this world.

1 John 4:17 - *Love has been perfected among us in this: that we may have boldness in the day of judgment; because as He is, so are we in this world.*

Christ was put to death instead of us, upon a cross / tree. Then in three days the Father raised Him from the dead; this brought us life. Just as Christ was resurrected, we too have been given the gift of new life.

1Peter 1:3 *Blessed be the God and Father of our Lord Jesus Christ, who according to His abundant mercy has begotten us again to a living hope through the resurrection of Jesus Christ from the dead.*

The Holy Spirit gives the enabling to heal the sick and work miracles when we see the Father doing them. Some can by the spirit, have supernatural knowledge and wisdom to function in ways that normally we would not be able to. Others are able to prophesy and speak to our Father in other tongues, an unknown language and on occasions interpret into a known language.

1 Corinthians 12:4,8-10 - *There are diversities of gifts, but the same Spirit .....*

8 for to one is given the word of wisdom through the Spirit, to another the word of knowledge through the same Spirit, to another faith by the same Spirit, to another gifts of healings by the same Spirit, to another the working of miracles, to another prophecy, to another discerning of spirits, to another different kinds of tongues, to another the interpretation of tongues.

The Holy Spirit has been given to help us to live good, fruitful new creation lives that the Father planned from the beginning. We have been delivered from the curse of the Tree of the Knowledge of good and evil and are restored by Jesus to New Life in the Kingdom that leads to the Tree of Life. May we live out this new life to the glory of our Father.

Mark 16:15,17-18 - *And He said to them, "Go into all the world and preach the gospel to every creature...... [17] And these signs will follow those who believe: In My name they will cast out demons; they will speak with new tongues; .... they will lay hands on the sick, and they will recover."*

Whatever you do in word or deed, do all in the name of the Lord Jesus, giving thanks to God the Father through Him.

Love Life, and be full of the peace and joy of the Lord, from this day forth and for evermore.
Amen

For more information contact Julie at - julie.a.m.andrews@gmail.com

This is the 5.5 x 8.5 Basic Template. Paste your manuscript into this template or simply start typing. Delete this text prior to use.

Printed in Poland
by Amazon Fulfillment
Poland Sp. z o.o., Wrocław

65421949R00034